IMAGES
of America

KINGSTON

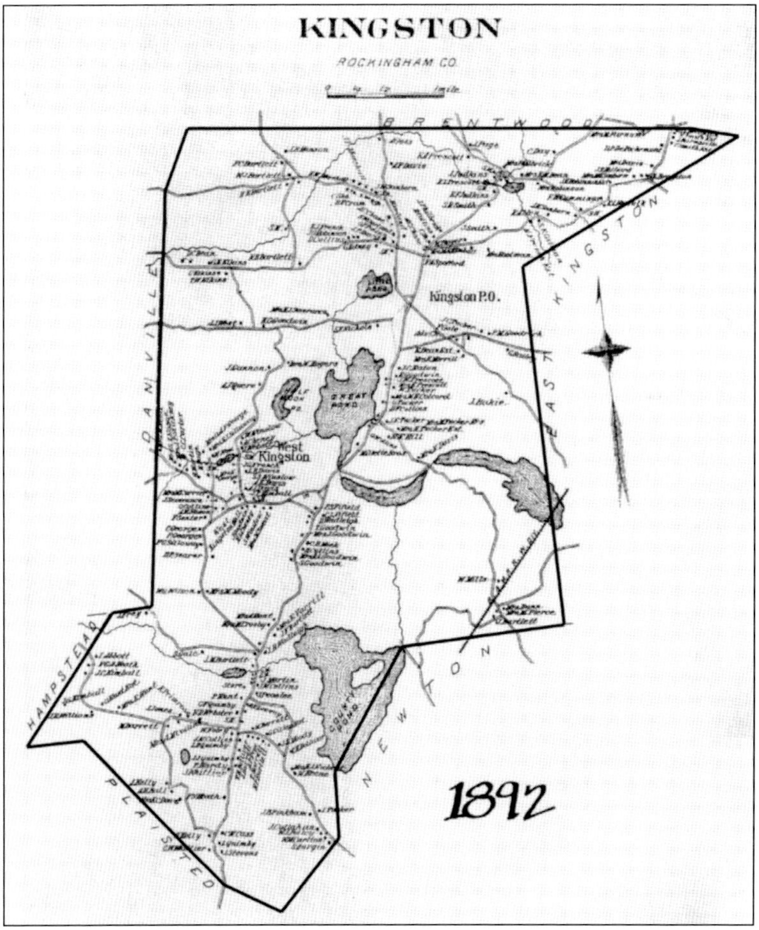

This 1892 map of Kingston shows the locations of early businesses and the homes of families with longstanding ties to Kingston. Great Pond (Kingston Lake) and Little Pond (Greenwood Pond) in the center of the map have provided residents with many leisure activities throughout the years. (Courtesy of the Kingston Historical Museum.)

On the Cover: The Kingston Brass Band was formed in 1875 and operated until 1884, when it was reorganized. During the initial nine years, the band practiced in the town hall building and performed concerts in the bandstand on the Plains. When the band reorganized as the Kingston Cornet Band in 1884, the members played concerts and paraded in Kingston or surrounding towns during holidays. This 1886 photograph shows the band in boats on Greenwood Pond, where they would travel around performing for residents enjoying the summer. The group disbanded in 1932 due to a lack of younger performers. The drum used by the Kingston Cornet Band can be seen today at the Kingston Historical Museum. (Courtesy of the Kingston Historical Museum.)

IMAGES
of America

KINGSTON

James J. Enright, Kalena J. Kelly-Rossop,
and Emma L. Williams

ARCADIA
PUBLISHING

ISBN 978-1-4671-0723-5

Published by Arcadia Publishing
Charleston, South Carolina

Printed in the United States of America

Library of Congress Control Number: 2021945159

For all general information, please contact Arcadia Publishing:
Telephone 843-853-2070
Fax 843-853-0044
E-mail sales@arcadiapublishing.com
For customer service and orders:
Toll-Free 1-888-313-2665

Visit us on the Internet at www.arcadiapublishing.com

To my wife, Nicole, and my sons Joseph, Thomas, and James.
–Jim

To all the ethnic cultures that helped create Kingston and whose history is not documented in Kingston's records.
–Kalena

To my family, friends, and those who helped me write, Diana and Linda.
–Emma

Contents

Acknowledgments

This book was a collaborative effort and would not have been possible without the support of many. The authors thank the staff at the Kingston Historical Museum for their tireless and endless support of this project. In particular, Lesley-Ann Hume and Walter Roy provided a tremendous amount of expertise regarding archival images, scanning, and historical knowledge to make this book possible. Their unwavering support is further evidenced considering that they made themselves available during a time when the museum was closed to the public due to the pandemic. The authors' proceeds from this book are being donated to the Kingston Historical Museum to support its mission of preserving Kingston's history.

We also thank acquisitions editor Erin L. Vosgien and title manager Caroline Anderson Vickerson of Arcadia Publishing. Erin provided a general direction for the book, and Caroline provided tremendous support and insight as we progressed through the writing process. Several Sanborn Regional High School individuals were instrumental in the writing of this book: as the English teacher for Kalena and Emma, Aaron Cass provided support and proofreading guidance; extended learning opportunity coordinator Kerrie Alley-Violette provided support and flexibility for us to write this book; and principal Brian Stack supported this endeavor from the first mention of the idea of two students and a teacher writing *Kingston*, as he makes great effort to provide students with many learning experiences to ensure their future success.

Finally, we thank our families who supported our desire to write a book about the local area. Sorting through images, writing captions, and meeting with the Kingston Historical Museum meant late nights, early mornings, and working during vacations. Our families were supportive and understanding.

We could not have done it without these individuals, so thank you!

Unless otherwise noted, all images appear courtesy of the Kingston Historical Museum.

INTRODUCTION

Kingston is a small New Hampshire town with a rich history. European settlement can be traced back to the time when the area was part of the Massachusetts colony, until 1692, when New Hampshire became a separate province. From 1638 until 1694, Kingston was a part of Hampton. During the nine years preceding incorporation, 12 people had accepted an offer of land at Great Pond, becoming the first European settlers of Kingston. In 1694, several Hampton residents petitioned the governor for township of the western lands of Hampton, thus forming Kingstown, the original name under which it was incorporated on August 6, 1694. Although the current Kingston boundaries have been in existence since the mid-1700s, their specific location was a source of great dispute among many of the present-day towns originally included in Kingston's charter, such as East Kingston, Danville, and Sandown. Kingston was established with a government of three selectmen, two constables, and a town clerk. A board of selectmen continues as the town's form of governance.

While Kingston was incorporated in 1694, its story starts much earlier. The Native American presence in the area is well documented in written history, if not in photographs. Historic Native American trails originating in the Haverhill, Massachusetts, area, traveled through Kingston and to Great Pond, known as Massapaug (meaning "many oaks"). These trails eventually led through the Seacoast area into Maine. Among the more common tribes in the area were the Algonquin, Abenaki, Pennacooks, Piscataqua, Pequawkets, Squamscot, and Winnecowet. Early European settlers learned a great deal from the Native Americans, including local agriculture, hunting, and building techniques. As a rural outpost along some of the primary trails, Kingston was more prone to conflict with the Native Americans, and tensions likely would have increased as the European population expanded in the region. Many Native American artifacts have been found locally by Kingston resident John Eaton. Other artifacts have been found along the Powwow River and in the Plains area. A collection of the artifacts found by Eaton can be seen at the Kingston Historical Museum.

From the beginnings of European settlement in Kingston through the mid-1800s, residents worked to establish themselves. While they were primarily engaged in farming, other industries also flourished in town. Sawmills were particularly important to build houses. As many as six sawmills operated on the waterways in Kingston during this period. Also situated along waterways, gristmills played an important role in grinding whole grains into flour for cooking. Tanneries provided residents with leather for clothing, shoes, and hats.

Nicknamed "the Carriage Towne" in 1875 due to the number of horse-drawn carriage builders, Kingston quickly established itself as a leading center for the carriage industry with businesses such as Walter S. Clark Carriage Shop, Cilley Carriage Shop, and the H.W. Marshall Carriage Co. selling carriages locally and in some cases across the country. With advancements in transportation, the horse-drawn carriage gave way to the automobile, and for a time, shoe factories sustained the local economy. In the 1920s, several poultry breeders established operations in Kingston, and

Christie Poultry Farms became the country's largest breeder for the boiler market. The Christie and Nichols poultry operations quickly made Kingston the center of the poultry industry. The Kingston breeders even developed their own breeds of chicken, and shipped poultry throughout the country and internationally. Christie's customers included widely known distributors of poultry products such as Tyson Foods.

In a time of changes in education, Kingston resident Maj. Edward S. Sanborn founded the Sanborn Seminary, which provided residents, as well as those from surrounding towns and states, with a high school education. Prior to 1942, elementary students in Kingston were educated in one of seven different one-room schoolhouses until a centralized school was built through a generous donation by Daniel J. Bakie. The Daniel J. Bakie Elementary School continues to operate after expansions and renovations, serving generations of Kingston's youth. The Sanborn Seminary was sold to the newly formed Sanborn Regional School District in 1966, and served as Sanborn Regional High School. Many of the original seminary campus buildings have been removed, and the remaining buildings have fallen into disrepair. A new high school was completed in 2006, and the seminary campus was sold to private developers in 2020. The seminary building remains a focal point of Kingston with its gothic architecture and surrounding wrought-iron fence.

Hard-working Kingston residents have also found time to enjoy national pastimes and the natural wonders surrounding the town. Along the shores of the lakes and ponds, day and overnight camps have provided plenty of opportunities for youth to boat, fish, swim, and camp. The Lone Tree Scout Reservation has been operating since 1949, hosting scouts from Kingston and neighboring communities. Kingston State Park was established on the shore of Great Pond in 1934 and offers many lakeside amenities to residents and visitors. In the winter months, Great Pond has been home to ice fishing, as well as ice racing for cars in the 1950s. Social clubs have also been a source of entertainment for residents since the late 1800s. The Kingston Coronet Band (shown on the cover), the Kingston Players, the Veterans Club, and the Masons, among other organizations, have long served as both sources of entertainment and as social networks for the community.

Kingston has also known tragedy. As residents of an outpost in the wilderness, early settlers were well aware of their vulnerability. Attacks from Native Americans in the undeveloped land were not uncommon. Even in times of peace, residents experienced death with the onset of the Great Throat Distemper of 1735, in which the first recorded death was a young child in Kingston. After the outbreak in Kingston, it spread across New Hampshire, north into Maine, and south into Massachusetts. It mostly affected children, many of whom died within three days of contracting it. The epidemic lasted until 1740 and claimed the lives of over 5,000 people. In New Hampshire, where it hit the hardest, 75 out of every 1,000 people died, nearly three quarters of whom were children.

But through the good times and tragedies, Kingston residents remained strong and proud of their history, which began as a settlement of a dozen people and continues into the 21st century with over 6,000 residents. Traditions are kept alive in celebrations, parades, and the annual Kingston Days. The town's history has been carefully documented through generous donations by residents. Documents, images, and artifacts are meticulously cataloged and available for viewing at the Kingston Historical Museum. The museum is comprised of several buildings and contains examples of the horse-drawn carriages once built here during the carriage building boom. Tours of the historic area of Kingston are also offered on various occasions.

One

Around Town

From old schools and carriage shops to the home of the second signer of the Declaration of Independence, the buildings in Kingston are more than brick and mortar or clapboard. Some are now long gone, others repaired, some even missing pieces. But their existence tells a story of the experiences and the lives of those who lived, worked, or played there. These are the memories that will last forever, even after the structures have long disappeared.

Along with the structures are the roads that hold them all together. The Kingston Plains contain some of the roads that connect the most well-known buildings in town. There are 75 buildings connected to the Plains, with grassy fields in between. These fields have seen many years of celebrations and events, including the annual Kingston Days celebration, as well as a place to hold recess for students at the Plains School or Sanborn Seminary. Today, families and friends frequent the Plains for various occasions. In the summer, many picnics are held under the trees while dogs play frisbee with their owners. The winter months bring kids to play in the snow and enjoy the peacefulness of Kingston.

Scattered throughout town are businesses where residents have long worked. As a hub of the carriage building industry, Kingston provided many of the horse-drawn carriages used throughout New Hampshire and New England. Advances in transportation eventually brought the carriage manufacturing days to an end, but Kingston residents kept pace with the changing times. Walter S. Clark was one of the pioneers who saw an opportunity in the face of adversity and expanded his business to bicycles, home fuel oil delivery, and automobile repair. Subsequent generations have continued the business to the present day.

The Bakie Brothers General Store on the corner of Main Street and Depot Road was opened in 1840 by Luther D. Peaslee as a general store. The third floor was added to the building in 1871 to support the Masonic lodge. The Bakie Brothers had operated another general store in Kingston before moving to this location in 1875. The store continued in operation by the Bakie family until 1960; however, the site continued as a general store for many years. Today, a flower shop and apartments are located in the building.

The 1919 Kingston celebration on the Plains brought together former and current residents. Here, looking west across the Plains, vehicles are parked for the events and activities, including a parade.

This early photograph of Main Street looks east toward Exeter. The unpaved roads show wagon wheel tracks, common before roads were clearly established and paved.

The First Universalist Church (now Church on the Plains) was designed by C. Willis Damon from Haverhill, Massachusetts, and built in 1879. The church was deconsecrated in 1954 and donated to the Kingston Improvement and Historical Society in 1974, then listed in the National Register of Historic Places in 1979. The historical society has meticulously maintained the church, and it remains available for special events such as weddings.

This early 1900s photograph shows a view of Church Street looking west from Main Street. On the left is the Congregational church. Across the street are the barn and icehouse of the Luther Dana Peaslee homestead. Peaslee built his house and general store on the corner of Main Street and Depot Road in the 1840s.

This northwest view of Depot Road shows early development along Church Street. The Masonic building is on the left, followed by the Methodist church. The Methodist and Congregational churches joined in 1917. The former church building has been used for several purposes, including Sanborn Seminary's first gymnasium. Today, it is home to the Kingston Children's Center, which provides year-round day care. On the right, behind the trees, the end of the Peaslee Park barn can be seen.

In 1889, members of the West Kingston Improvement Association voted to purchase land for the construction of a building to be used for community activities. The West Kingston Union Hall was completed in 1892 to be used "for all good and moral purposes." Throughout the years, it was used for 4-H clubs, the grange, church services, and social events, including parties for residents entering the armed forces.

This view looking north toward Church Street from Depot Road shows the back of Peaslee's store, where general merchandise such as dry goods and canned foods were sold along with household and farm supplies. Peaslee's store was built in 1845 and became the Bakie Brothers General Store in 1875. In the background is the Methodist church. On the right behind the trees is the Peaslee homestead, some of which later became the site of Nichols Memorial Library, the current location of the Kingston Historical Museum.

The H.W. Marshall Carriage Co. was one of many carriage manufacturers in Kingston. The large concentration of carriage manufacturers led to Kingston being declared "the Carriage Towne" in 1875. Many carriage manufacturers also sold accessories, including blankets, robes, and harnesses. Herbert W. Marshall sold carriages wholesale and created a sales brochure showing images of the models he offered, such as the small one pictured below. Carriages like this cost between $150 and $200 at the time. Marshall traveled throughout the country taking orders.

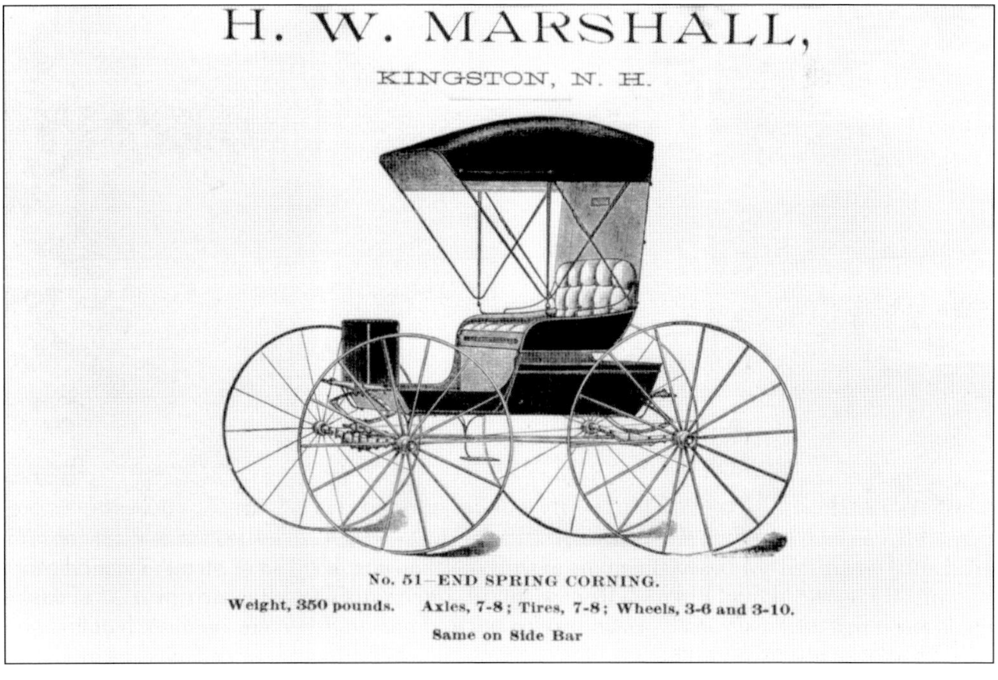

The Greenwood Lake Lodge on Church Street was built as a hotel and restaurant just outside of the center of Kingston. It was converted to apartments in the 1970s.

The Nason Store was on the corner of Main Street and Bartlett Road. The store building was originally built by Levi Bartlett. It was known as Webster's Store and the Henry French Store. Irving Nason purchased the property in 1919. The general store closed in the early 1970s and the building later became the location for several other businesses, including Little John's Bar and Swiss House. It is currently operating as Rick's Cafe.

Among the many Kingston businesses in operation in the early part of the 1900s was the G.H. Emery Store, built in 1902. George H. Emery sold groceries, but not feed. His daughter Evy married Irving Nason and helped run the Nason Store. As was common at the time, these stores sold dry goods, canned food, and household supplies.

The Kingston Post Office was on the right side of this building from the 1920s through the 1940s. David Brewer operated a store on the left, which was run by Arthur and Mildred Tucker in the 1940s. Elmer and Gladys Larson purchased the property, which was used for several businesses including a furniture store until it was torn down in 1968.

Prior to the present town hall building, the previous town hall (above) was in the Kingston Wesleyan Academy building overlooking the Plains, which was built by the Methodist church in 1819. The town assumed ownership of the building and lot in 1856 and used it as the town hall while the academy continued until 1900. The building was destroyed by fire in 1928 (below). The present town hall was erected on the same site in 1929. It continues to operate in the same location as the original building overlooking the Plains.

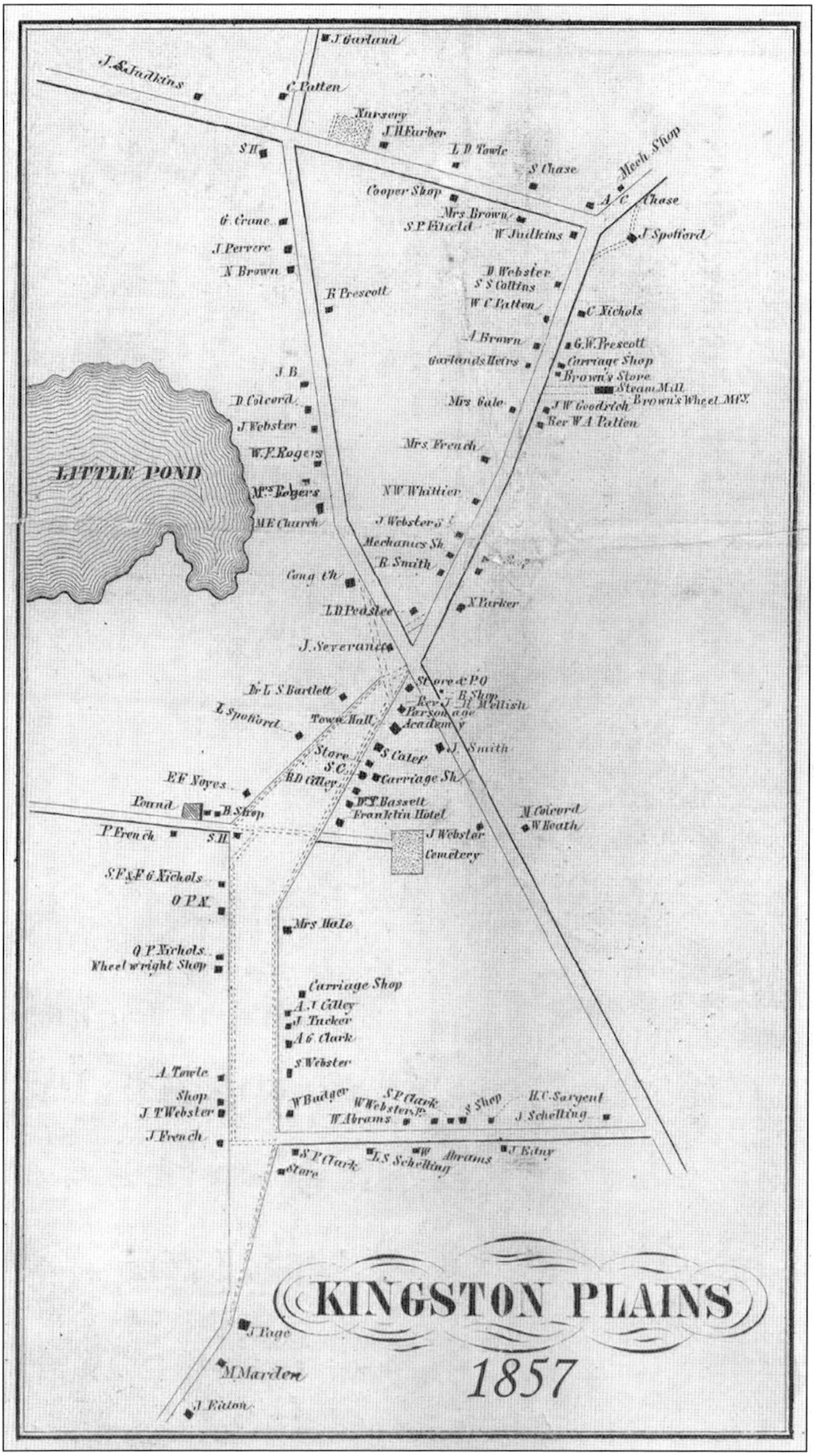

Kingston's major roads, as seen in this 1857 map, remain to the present day. At the top is Chase Street, and Church Street is to the right of Little Pond. The home of Josiah Bartlett is to the left of the Plains. At center is the Plains Cemetery. Bartlett Street runs along the bottom.

Published by Bakie Bros. Old Grist Mill, Little River, Kingston, N. H. Hand Colored

Kingston had several gristmills in operation starting from the early 1700s and lasting until the 1890s. One of the gristmills with the longest continuous operation in Kingston was Judkin's Grist Mill on Little River Road, which was in operation until the 1940s.

The Liberty Elms received their name after tea from the Boston Tea Party was reportedly burned under them. The trees were on Main Street in front of Al and Christine (Conant) Moores' home. The Moores operated a hardware store in a building to the left of the residence. After changes in ownership, the building came to house Kingston Insurance Agency.

The Congregational church at 6 Church Street is seen here looking north from Main Street at the end of the Plains. The church was built in 1825 and remodeled in 1840. A parsonage was built in 1954. Additional renovations and expansions took place several times; the most recent addition was in 2013.

At the corner of Main Street and Depot Road, Nichols Memorial Library (left) and the Bakie Brothers General Store still remain where they stood over 100 years ago. The Bakie Brothers General Store building also once housed the Kingston Post Office. Both buildings were in the center of town along Main Street.

Although technically part of Kingston, the area to the west known as West Kingston functioned as its own community. The lumber industry was an important business here, with two sawmills operated by the Page family on land provided through a grant from the king of England. On the right is the West Kingston School (District No. 4).

Cornish's and the Do Drop Inn restaurants were in the center of Kingston at 165 Main Street until the early 1970s. The building stood to the right of Bakie Brothers General Store, in front of the Grace Daly house. In 1972, the restaurant closed and the building was demolished.

Kingston Outboard in Kingston Plaza began operating in 1957. The original owners were Ed McAskill Sr., Ed McAskill Jr., and Ed Stempian. The business was open for a total of 13 years before closing in 1970. After it closed, the plaza was divided into several different businesses. The plaza is still around today and brings many people to its busy location on Main Street.

Peaslee Park at 172 Main Street was built in 1840 by Luther Dana Peasley. The Greek Revival house has five bedrooms and a 1.3-acre yard. Peaslee also built the general store across the street from the house using a similar style.

The Plains area was first cleared by Native Americans who occupied the area as early as 8,000 years ago. Early settlers used the space for commerce and as a location for Kingston's first meeting house. The crossroads are seen here looking west toward South Kingston.

Harry "Whiskers" Clark photographed much of Kingston in the early to mid-1900s. In the summers, he set up two tents on the Plains next to the bandstand, where he took photographs and sold ice cream. Many of the pictures in this book were taken by him.

The Cobbler Shop was built sometime in the 1800s. Kingston's Arthur Reynolds purchased the shop from the Frank Allard estate in Danville and moved it to his home on Main Street next to his antique barn, where it is pictured. Reynolds sold the shop, and it was moved to Kensington. The Kingston Historical Museum purchased it, and it is currently located next to town hall. Inside, tools are lying on the workbench and hanging on the walls, where many shoes and shoe parts were made by Kingston residents.

As the highest point in Kingston in the early 1900s, the Sanborn Seminary tower offered a tremendous view of the surrounding area. This is a northwest view of Church Street. Patten School can be seen on North Road, and Chase Street is on the left. The Patten family lived in the home at the corner of North Road and Church Street.

The first gathering of the Church of Christ took place on September 17, 1725, at the meeting house on the Plains. The First Congregational Church, seen here, was constructed in 1825 and renovated in 1875. Renovations stopped until the 1950s, when the sanctuary was renovated and the Rent Room and parsonage were added. The carillon was installed in 1986, playing Westminster bells on the hour. Looking from left to right down Church Street, Kingston's First Congregational Church, Masonic building, and at the end, the Methodist church and parsonage, can be seen. The First Congregational Church is still in use today.

This view to the northeast was taken from atop the Sanborn Seminary tower. Running through the center is Main Street, which leads to Exeter to the left. The building on the left in the foreground was home to Sanborn Seminary's home economics classes in the 1950s. The home and barn on the right were the Sanborn Seminary principal's residence.

In the late 1800s, the Kingston House (above) at 175 Main Street operated as a local inn on a major route between New Hampshire and Massachusetts. The old hotel also operated as a tavern. In 1902, guests paid $2 per day or $9–12 per week. There was room for 25 guests, and it was open year-round. By the early 1900s, Thomas Tracy's barbershop, below, was built alongside.

On Main Street next to the Kingston House, Thomas Tracy's barbershop provided barber services to residents and visitors in the late 1800s and early 1900s. A striped barber pole can be seen in front of the shop in this image from the late 1800s. The barbershop was eventually torn down as Sanborn Seminary expanded and Kingston House was acquired.

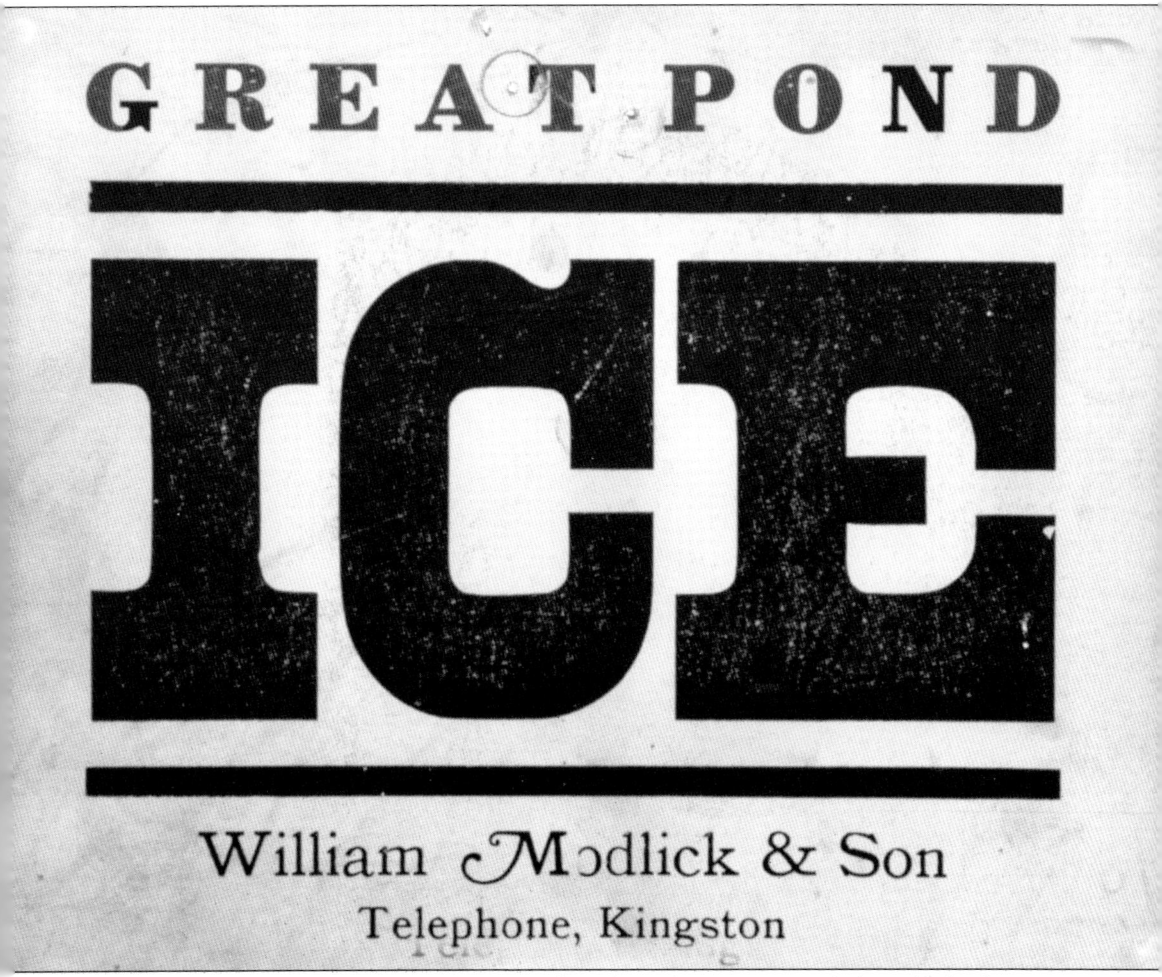

The Great Pond Ice company, which operated in the early 1900s, provided ice for food storage to Kingston and other local areas. The ice was delivered by horse and buggy to customers on the route. With refrigerators becoming more common beginning in the 1940s, Great Pond Ice went out of business in the 1950s.

Looking east from the Sanborn Seminary tower in this early 1900s photograph, the principal's house is on the left. The land across Main Street was formerly part of the Josiah Bartlett farm but became the location for the Daniel J. Bakie Elementary School in 1941. The seminary driveway entry arch showing four granite columns, two of which support the iron arch, can be seen on Main Street with three Sanborn baseball players standing under it. Eventually, the two inner columns were removed to allow buses to enter the school grounds. Later arches were supported by the two outer blocks.

Shown in the early 1900s above and during the 1919 Kingston celebration below, Nichols Memorial Library was built in 1898 by J. Howard Nichols and donated to the town. For four years prior to the construction of this building, the library was housed in the selectmen's room of the town hall. The building was listed in the National Register of Historic Places in 1981 and served as the town's library until 2012, when a new one was built. Since 2012, Nichols Memorial Library has housed the Kingston Historical Museum.

When Walter S. Clark was 15 years old, he opened a blacksmith shop, which later turned into a more well-known carriage and bicycle shop, as well as a car dealership in 1904. In 1932, it expanded into an auto repair shop and, until recently, a heating fuel company. Pictured here in the 1880s from left to right are Charles Leach, Helen Clark, Marion Clark, and Walter S. Clark.

This early 1900s view shows the Universalist church (Church on the Plains) and the Franklin Hotel. The Franklin Hotel was built in 1760 by John Calef Sr. as a three-story building. The Cape-style addition was added in 1810. The Franklin Hotel was also known as the Frost Hotel and Ye Olde Kingston Inn. The Frost Hotel continued to operate through a succession of owners until William Bartlett Jr. purchased it in 1966. During this time, it was often referred to as the "Old Hotel" or the "Old Kingston Inn." Bartlett closed the hotel and had the third floor removed in 1967. Today, the entire building is occupied by Merrill Bartlett Group Real Estate. The Church on the Plains remains in place today.

On the corner of Bartlett and Main Streets and overlooking the Plains, Levi Bartlett operated a small general store providing general merchandise, canned goods, and other products. Taken in the early 1900s, this photograph shows the fenced enclosure behind the building. This building later became Webster's Store, the Henry French Store, the Nason Store, and eventually Rick's Cafe, which stands today.

This southern view of Church Street from atop the Sanborn Seminary tower shows Josiah Bartlett's house and farm on the left. In the foreground of the Bartlett homestead is Judge Louis G. Hoyt's law office. The Congregational church is at center, and the Masonic building is to the right. The Plains are to the left of the Bartlett homestead, just outside of this picture.

This is a postcard of Vinehurst, built in 1840 at 134 Main Street. Vinehurst was occupied by Judge Louis G. Hoyt from about 1900 until the 1930s. Judge Hoyt added the porte cochere entryway, although the addition was removed by later owners. Judge Hoyt is believed to have been the first Kingston resident to own an automobile. (Courtesy of James Enright.)

Peaslee Park, seen on the left in this early 1900s view looking north up Main Street from the Bakie Bros. Store toward Sanborn Seminary, was built in 1840. Luther Dana Peaslee built the house at the same time as the Kingston general store that he originally owned but later sold to Bakie Brothers in 1875. At far right is the Larson House (built around 1800), and at center is the Jones House (built around 1810). In the foreground on the right is a gas-lantern street light with a street lighter's ladder. The streetlight pole is still standing in front of Nichols Memorial Library.

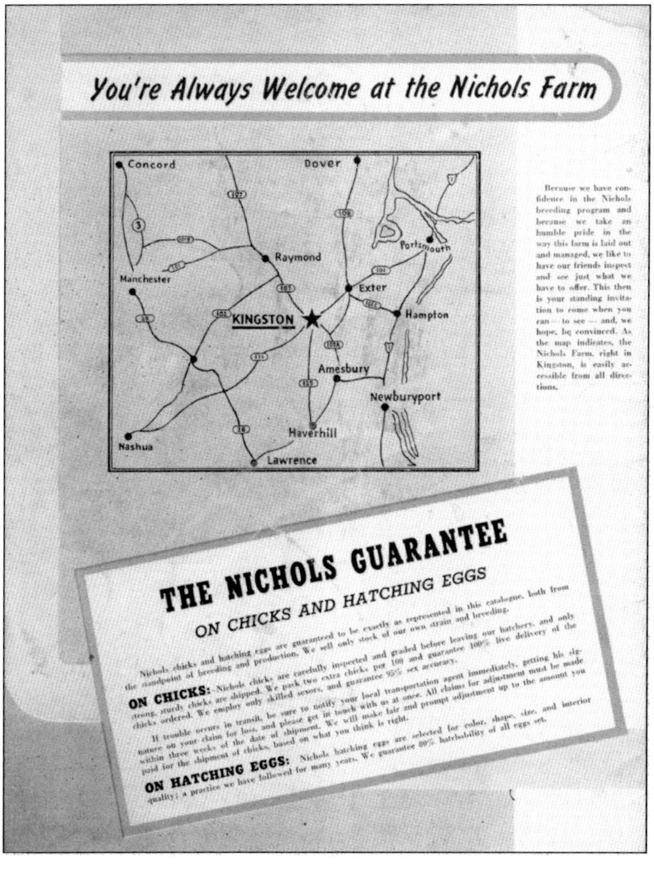

In the first half of the 1900s, Kingston became a center for the poultry business, with several poultry farms operating here and in several locations throughout New Hampshire. Nichols Poultry Farm, shown above in 1954, had its primary operations on Rockrimmon Road. The farm housed 18,000 birds.

Built in 1929 after the previous town hall was destroyed by fire, the current town hall was built on the same site as the original building. It continues to operate in the same location overlooking the Plains.

Buzzell's Grove, operating as a store with seasonal cottages for rent, was in business from the 1940s until the 1970s. The store was accessible from both the road and Great Pond. Located on Main Street, opposite the intersection of New Boston Road, customers could purchase groceries, candy, and other items. Buzzell's Grove was sold to the Alhmen family and renamed Chriskel's Grove and variety, after their children Christopher and Kelly. (Courtesy of James Enright.)

Published by Bakie Bros. On the Powwow Road to Kingston. N. H.

This early 1900s postcard of Powwow Road in Kingston shows the Bakie Farm. The trees lining the road were planted by the Bakie brothers. The Bakie family continuously operated the farm for 144 years until John Bakie passed away in 1997. In 2018, the farm was purchased and became the Bakie Farm Initiative, an educational farm. Existing buildings are being restored, and sustainable farming practices are implemented. (Courtesy of James Enright.)

The Daniel J. Bakie Elementary School was built through a generous $15,000 donation by Daniel J. Bakie, who placed an additional $15,000 in a trust to provide for future maintenance and expansion. The construction of the school allowed Kingston's five district schools, all of which were in varying states of disrepair, to combine into a single elementary school bringing children from all around Kingston to one location.

This postcard of the Plains shows Kingston's village green area. On the right is the Bakie Brothers General Store prior to the side addition. Peaslee Park can be seen through the trees at center, with the Larson home beyond. Main Street is seen here before roads were paved. Fencing along the Plains was important to keep grazing animals inside the village green area and out of people's yards. (Courtesy of James Enright.)

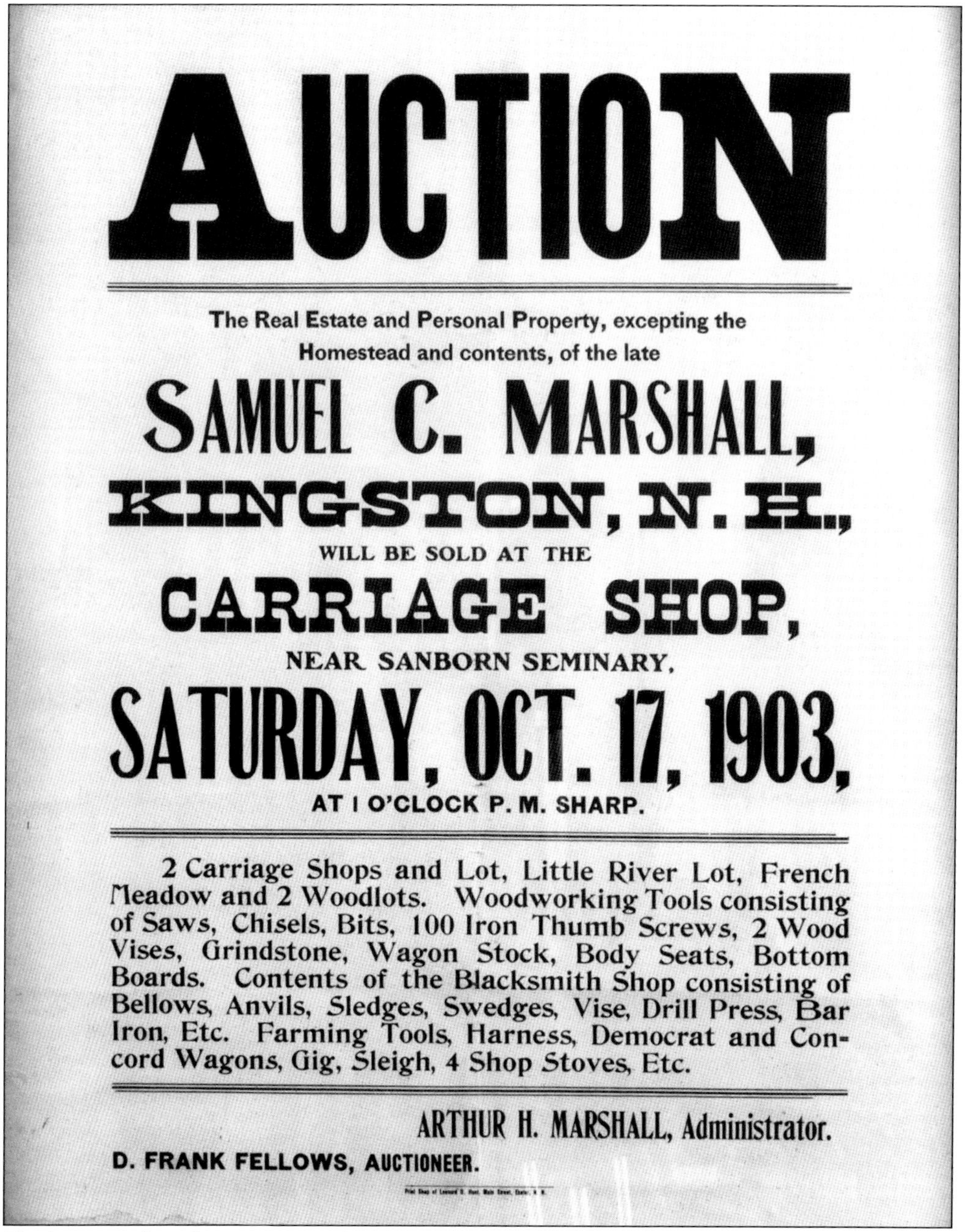

AUCTION

The Real Estate and Personal Property, excepting the Homestead and contents, of the late

SAMUEL C. MARSHALL, KINGSTON, N. H.,

WILL BE SOLD AT THE

CARRIAGE SHOP,

NEAR SANBORN SEMINARY,

SATURDAY, OCT. 17, 1903,

AT 1 O'CLOCK P. M. SHARP.

2 Carriage Shops and Lot, Little River Lot, French Meadow and 2 Woodlots. Woodworking Tools consisting of Saws, Chisels, Bits, 100 Iron Thumb Screws, 2 Wood Vises, Grindstone, Wagon Stock, Body Seats, Bottom Boards. Contents of the Blacksmith Shop consisting of Bellows, Anvils, Sledges, Swedges, Vise, Drill Press, Bar Iron, Etc. Farming Tools, Harness, Democrat and Concord Wagons, Gig, Sleigh, 4 Shop Stoves, Etc.

ARTHUR H. MARSHALL, Administrator.

D. FRANK FELLOWS, AUCTIONEER.

The large number of carriage manufacturers in Kingston, combined with the impending increase in automobile usage, led to several carriage manufacturers having to change their business direction or close completely. In 1903, following the death of Samuel C. Marshall, the Marshall Carriage Shop liquidated all assets related to carriage building.

In desperate need of a modern firehouse to store equipment, Kingston approved the construction of a firehouse on the site of the Plains School in 1949. Prior to the construction of the new station, fire equipment was stored in the 1885 firehouse, and starting in 1930, in the two bays below town hall. Additional equipment purchased in 1958 and 1959 led to an addition to the central firehouse in 1968.

The S. Hoyt House, shown here in the late 1890s, was built in 1846 and later occupied by Otis Tucker, a civil war soldier from Kingston who died in 1890. Many Tucker family members still live in Kingston. The house, at 84A Main Street, was next to Judge Hoyt's summer cottage on Great Pond.

By 1932, when this photograph was taken of owner and operator Edward B. Clark (left) and his brother-in-law George Stevens, Walter S. Clark and Sons was operating as an automobile garage and service station, although the location remained the same as when horse-drawn carriages were being built 50 years earlier. In addition to auto service and repair, Clark also offered home fuel oil delivery.

In the mid-1930s, Walter S. Clark and Sons had expanded to include a 1934 Chevrolet fuel truck. The vehicle, seen driven by Gardner Conant, had a 725-gallon capacity, which could hold plenty of fuel oil to meet the demand of residents of Kingston and the surrounding area.

The shores of "Little Pond" (Greenwood Pond) were frequently used for fishing or launching boats, as seen in this early 1900s postcard. Easily accessible from Church Street, Greenwood Pond offered residents many fishing and boating opportunities. Some even left their boats along the shore for later use.

On the shore of Great Pond, Bolton's Drive-In, shown here in 1969, offered walk-up service for patrons to order food and eat at one of the picnic tables. Bolton's remains in the same location but is a sit-down restaurant offering inside as well as outside deck seating overlooking the pond.

As seen in this 1910 postcard view of Main Street looking north toward Sanborn Seminary, horse-drawn carriages were the most popular method of transportation based on the wagon wheel tracks. The fence along the Plains remained for many years after this photograph was taken.

This early 1900s postcard shows the Josiah Bartlett homestead at 156 Main Street. It was originally built in 1751 by Josiah Bartlett, but was destroyed by a fire set by British loyalists due to Bartlett's support for independence. After the fire, Bartlett built the current primary part of the house in 1774. In the mid-1800s, the 2.5-story wood structure was renovated in Greek Revival style, and a two-story addition was built on the back. The wide plank floors and post-and-beam construction were all made from local timber. The home was listed in the National Register of Historic Places in 1971.

Hotel Lake View operated in South Kingston in the late 1890s into the early 1900s. The hotel was operated by owners Sanborn and Leboux. This photograph was likely taken in the late 1890s shortly after its opening.

Annie Tucker's Bathing Beach, shown here in the 1930s or early 1940s, was on the shore of Great Pond. Swimming, diving boards, and a bathhouse were available to patrons, who paid 10¢ to park. Tucker also operated the store at left, selling candy, soda, cigarettes, and other small items.

This late 1920s postcard of Badger's Corner shows where Badger Tavern once stood on the corner of Main Street and Scotland Road. William and Elizabeth Badger opened the tavern in the early 1800s along what was once a highly traveled road between New Hampshire and Massachusetts. As a popular route for travelers, this stretch of Kingston was home to many taverns and inns. Badger Tavern stood until 1921, when it was razed. The marker shown here served as the only evidence of its existence. The land remained undeveloped until 2020, when new construction for a home began.

This image of the Plains as they appeared in 1908 looking north toward Depot Road shows the bandstand on the right and the Josiah Bartlett homestead on the left. In the right background is the Bakie Brothers General Store. Fences around sections of the Plains and the Bartlett homestead were to keep wandering farm animals from damaging property.

Two

SANBORN SEMINARY

Secondary education in Kingston has its formal roots in the Sanborn Seminary. Built and founded in 1883 through a donation by Maj. Edward Stevens Sanborn, Sanborn Seminary graduated its first class in 1890. At its start, the seminary consisted of four classes: junior, junior middle, senior middle, and senior. A fifth-grade preparatory class was also established for a short period for students needing additional training from grammar school. Students attending Sanborn Seminary lived in Kingston as well as surrounding towns, including Newton, Plaistow, Derry, and East Kingston.

Sanborn Seminary continued to grow, and in 1890 added a boys' dormitory for residential students. The former Kingston Hotel, across Main Street from the seminary campus, was acquired and named first Kingston Hall and then Wiggin Hall. As the seminary expanded, the number of buildings on campus increased, and in 1913, Colcord Hall was built through the generosity of Elihu W. Colcord. This new building became a girls' dormitory and dining hall. Following his death in 1920, William M. Gilmore bequeathed his 1880 home to the seminary, and it was promptly named Gilmore Cottage. The former French House built in 1800 became the principal's house.

As Kingston's population increased, Sanborn Seminary's growth was evident through campus expansions, including additional athletic fields (1925), an industrial arts building (1951), Swasey Gymnasium (1959), and the Science Building (1966). In 1962, the seminary's second-floor chapel, known as Seminary Hall, was converted to house the school's business department and a faculty lounge. In 1955, the decision was made to end boarding. Colcord Hall was converted from a girls' dormitory to classrooms, and Wiggin Hall was converted to a teachers' residence. The French House eventually became the office of the superintendent of the Sanborn Regional School District.

In 1966, due to the increasing number of high school students, the trustees of Sanborn Seminary voted to sell the campus to the Sanborn Regional School District, consisting of the towns of Kingston and Newton. On March 15, 1984, the seminary building was listed in the National Register of Historic Places as an example of New Hampshire's high Victorian gothic architecture.

EDWARD S. SANBORN, FOUNDER OF SANBORN SEMINARY.

Born Nov. 9, 1819, at Kingston, New Hampshire.

Trustee of Sanborn Seminary from Aug. 18, 1883, to Sept. 4, 1885.

Maj. Edward Stevens Sanborn, founder of the Sanborn Seminary, was born on November 9, 1819, and lived most of his early life in Kingston. He took his inheritance to Boston in search of new business opportunities, but later returned, becoming part of the New Hampshire state legislature. Once he had generated more wealth, he put $50,000 toward creating Sanborn Seminary. He gave $55,000 for the construction of the seminary building. Upon his death, he left an endowment of $250,000 to the school.

Following a serious illness in 1881, Major Sanborn rewrote his will and decided to build a private, coeducational high school in Kingston. In 1883, the school was built, and by 1888, Sanborn Seminary opened as a boarding school on Main Street. In the following years, while remaining a private school, the seminary contracted with local towns to accept their high school students. Sanborn Seminary became the high school for nine communities in New Hampshire.

The Sanborn Seminary was built in 1883 by Maj. Edward Stevens Sanborn and is listed in the National Register of Historic Places. The architect is unknown but the building clearly incorporates a Victorian gothic style.

Sanborn Seminary graduated its first class in 1890. Mary Webster, shown here in her graduation picture, graduated in 1897. The seminary originally had four classes: junior, junior middle, senior middle, and senior. A fifth class, known as the preparatory class for students completing additional academic class work to qualify to attend high school, existed for a few years but was later ended.

Members of the 1911 preparatory class include, from left to right, (first row) ? Smith, Florence Flanders, and Doris McFadden; (second row) Ella Lyford, Alice Powell, Ray McComb, ? Nason, and unidentified; (third row) Preston Lyford, Ruth Barrett, R. Stevens, and two unidentified; (fourth row) unidentified, Dorothy Eaton, ? Yeaton, John Brown, and ? Cheney.

PHYSICAL LABORATORY.

The science laboratory classrooms in the Sanborn Seminary were equipped with apparatus considered to be modern at the time. The physical science laboratory (above) contained equipment necessary to study the physical sciences. The chemistry laboratory (below) housed chemicals, burners, and other equipment necessary to study chemistry. In 1966, the Sanborn Regional School District added a new facility that included modern science classrooms and a library.

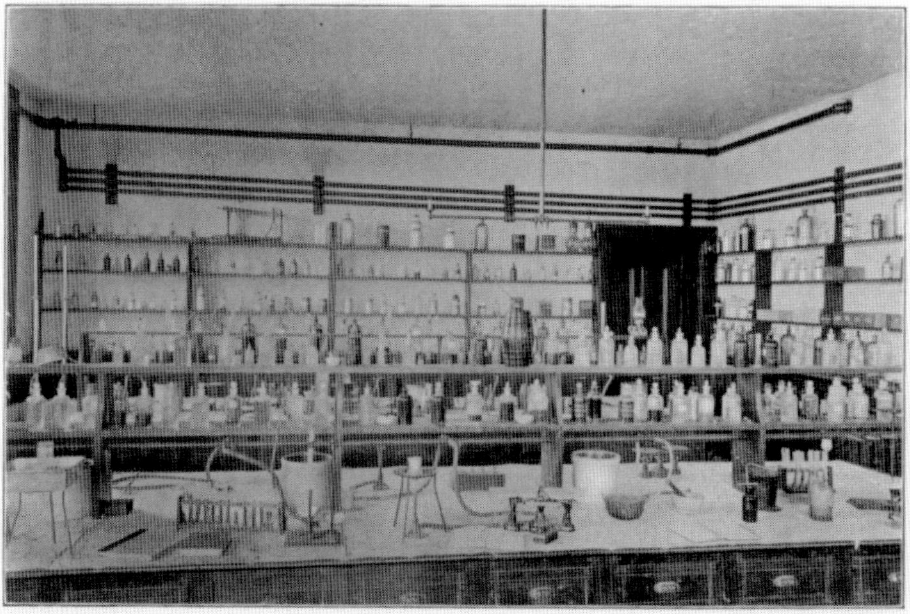

CHEMICAL LABORATORY.

ENTRANCE

The original entryway to Sanborn Seminary was built in 1883 and still stands as the front entrance of the building. Granite columns support the granite entrance porch. The front steps were used for graduation and team photographs for much of the seminary's first 50 years, with the exception of a few years when some team pictures were taken in front of Nichols Memorial Library.

The 1926 Sanborn Seminary football team shown here on the front steps of the seminary building included, from left to right, (first row) Skeet Ray, Jim Copadis, and unidentified; (second row) unidentified, Bob Swallow, Bill Bonner, Bill Cadso, and coach Pete Grant; (third row) unidentified, Fred Quimby, Chick Arnold, Ben Barker, Tubby Stone, Maurice Kimball, and Don Sabin; (fourth row) Biff Currier, Medie Beaulieau, and unidentified.

A pitcher for Sanborn Seminary takes the mound during a game at Chase Field. The athletic fields at the end of Church Street were home to Sanborn's many boys' and girls' teams and continue to be used today as additional athletic fields for Sanborn Regional High School.

Among the many sports at Sanborn Seminary, field hockey was a popular choice for girls. The field hockey team of 1950, shown here at Chase Field, competed against other local schools.

The Industrial Building was added to the seminary campus in 1951. The expansion enabled students to participate in elective courses that were not previously available. These students working on a car in the late 1960s are, from left to right, Stephen Fuller, Freddy Pitkin, Ulysses Wilson, and Al Walker.

Students pose in front of the bust of Major Sanborn in the entry foyer to Sanborn Seminary. The bust was commissioned by Sanborn while the seminary was being constructed and was placed in the entry foyer until moved to its current location in the new Sanborn Regional High School library in 2018.

In addition to the many other sports available at Sanborn Seminary, the cross-country team offered a competitive running program. This 1950s team picture shows the popularity of the sport.

Increasing student enrollment meant common areas were utilized for a multitude of purposes. In the 1940s, band practice was typically held in a classroom. Concerts were often held at the Kingston town hall prior to the construction of Swasey Gym in 1959. Depending on the event, either the stage or floor space was used.

The 1951 Sanborn Seminary production of *The Pirates of Penzance* held at town hall featured a primary cast of Robert Davis, David Conant, Henry Cornell, Richard Towne, John Wall, Lola Ward, Laqueita Peck, Bertha Carter, Judy Conant, Eugene Libby, and Janet Kemp. The musical production was accompanied by the school band, led by director Edward Dale.

Shown here in 1950 are members of the Sanborn Seminary cheerleading team at Chase field. From left to right are Norma Simes, Betty Bassett, and Doris Malaaf. The field is a short walk from the seminary campus on the corner of Chase and Church Streets. It is still used today for multiple sports, despite its distance from the new high school.

Sanborn Seminary, shown here in 1908, enjoyed a small, quiet campus on Main Street in Kingston. With its granite entryway and tree-lined driveway, the seminary building was the symbol of the Sanborn Regional School District until the new high school was completed in 2006. The building was sold to a developer in 2020.

DEAR OLD SANBORN

RUSSELL HILLIARD

I

The sun, the moon, and the stars above,
Give light and life to man;
They shape his way and guide his step;
His years their courses span.
More potent far than sun, or moon,
Or stars in Vaulted Blue
To us — today, and for all time,
Is Dear Old Sanborn true.

II

Her precincts, courts, her halls of lore,
Her ways and walks inspire;
A Beacon-Light, she leads us on;
Her flame, Celestial fire.
'Twas here we found companionship,
'Twas here close friendships made,
'Twas here we learned to give and take,
— The web of life to braid.

III

In years to come — when honors crowd,
Achievements bring acclaim,
When fretting care our spirits chafe,
When sorrow bites with pain,
Our hearts for praise, consoling grace,
To Sanborn will return;
As child maternal comfort craves,
For Sanborn we will yearn.

IV

Our lives may lead us far afield,
— From pole to pole may roam,
Our hearts united here will dwell,
Commune, and be at home.
The sun, the moon, and stars may fall,
And Chaos loose its chains,
This grey old earth will roll along,
While Sanborn still remains.

Refrain

Three cheers for Alma Mater, dear,
Three cheers for teachers call,
Three cheers for comrades — friends of youth,
God bless and save us all.

The music to "Dear Old Sanborn" was written by Russell Hilliard, class of 1946, and presented to Sanborn Seminary during his senior year. The lyrics were written by Enoch Pearson, Hilliard's piano teacher. The words and music were lost for many years, but recently, the school has resumed playing it at every graduation ceremony.

Sanborn Seminary had an active athletic department that included many boys' and girls' teams. In this 1940s photograph of Stan Bunker (left) and Harvey Steel, Sanborn Seminary's athletic fields at Chase Field are in the background. The initial athletic fields were considerably smaller until adjacent land was acquired. Chase Field continues to be used by Sanborn Regional High School.

Sitting atop the Sanborn Seminary for nearly 80 years, the bell tower was removed in August 1963 and placed on the side lawn. The bell was later moved to the front of the new Sanborn Regional High School. It is made of iron and weighs approximately 600 pounds. Unfortunately, having sat for over 40 years, the brittle bell sustained two cracks in its side. It now serves as a monumental piece for all Sanborn students, rung twice during their high school tenure: first on their first day of high school, and again on their graduation day.

The 1938 graduating class of Sanborn Seminary is shown on the front steps of the seminary building. From left to right are (first row) Vera Wilson, Evalyn Whitten, Eleanor Snow, Gertrude Lang, Bob Marshall, Makel Barenes, Barbara George, Winifred Carter, and Muriel LaTourette; (second row) Gladys Currier, Joan Andreurs, Beryl Marcotte, Helen Bean, Dorothy MacDougall, Gertrude Kershaw, Dorothy Thoreau, Rita Cavaric, and Lillian Cowell; (third row) principal Roy Hoyt, Louise Griffin, Olive Towle, Beatrice Woodworth, Kay Wilbur, Virginia Bennett, George Towle, Hal Whittier, and class advisor Jesse Flansbury; (fourth row) John Shippee, Eddie Snow, Ham St. Laurent, Charlene Hall, Leslie Pelley, Maklon Collins, Alfred Ellyson, and Charlie Friend; (fifth row) Walter Webster, Tom Houlihan, Charlie Shortle, Arthur Lessard, Bob Rowe, Dave Acox, and Harvey Seel; (sixth row) Lawrence Cheney, Alden Rollins, Willis Smith, Dick Demaine, and Dana Austin.

In addition to the variety of sports available at Sanborn Seminary, other extracurricular activities were available, including the debate team. Shown here are members of the 1944–1945 team (from left to right), James Mahoney, Eileen Little, Allen Warrington, Persis Blair, and Philip Wheaton.

SEMINARY HALL.

Seminary Hall in the seminary building served many purposes, including school and class assemblies as well as plays put on by Sanborn students. This picture from the 1907 *Sanborn Echo* shows the ornate detail in the formal hall. Seminary Hall was transformed into areas for music and classes as enrollment continued to increase and space became more limited.

Originally operating as the Kingston House Hotel, Wiggin Hall was purchased by the Sanborn Seminary in 1890. It was used as a boys' dormitory from 1890 until 1955, when it was transformed into a teachers' residence during Stewart McCormack's administration. It still stands today at 175 Main Street.

In June 1955, construction began on the new Swasey Gymnasium on the seminary campus. After taking nearly four years to complete, the new building was dedicated on January 4, 1959. John F. Swasey was a seminary trustee and a strong proponent of athletics at the school. The new gymnasium provided the seminary with much more space and an updated sports facility, replacing the previous gymnasium that had occupied the former Methodist church since 1925, when Swasey purchased the building.

GIRLS' DORMITORY SANBORN SEMINARY, KINGSTON, N. H.

Colcord Hall was built in 1913 through the generosity of Elihu W. Colcord. It was heated through steam and contained electric lights and bathrooms. It served as a girls' dormitory until 1955, when it was converted to classrooms. It was again repurposed in 1980, when the school administrative offices moved from the seminary. Having fallen into disrepair, Colcord Hall was demolished in 2011.

Published by Bakie Bros. Sanborn Seminary and Colcord Hall, Kingston, N. H. Hand Colored

The Sanborn Seminary student body of 1895 gathers on the front steps. Typical of the era, the women are wearing wear long, bell-shaped skirts that ended at the ankle, while the men are wearing jackets and ties. At this time, the school had only been open seven years.

This is one of the oldest known photographs of Sanborn Seminary, taken in 1890 by Newton resident Amos Jerome Burbeck. At the time, the school had been in operation for seven years and the first class had just graduated.

The 1944 Sanborn girls' basketball team included, from left to right, (first row) Joan Walters, Jean Tilton, Frannie Brown, Kay Cressy, Marjorie Long, and Shirley Brown; (second row) coach ? Wilson, Lois Milbury, Dorothy Miron, Frances Bird, Barbara Smith, Betty Sanborn, Persis Blair, Mary Ricker, and manager Pat Braley.

From the shores of Greenwood Pond close to the Plains, the steeples of the First Congregational Church (left) and Sanborn Seminary (right) can be seen in this early 1900s hand-colored postcard. (Courtesy of James Enright.)

Formerly known as the French House, the Sanborn Seminary principal's house was built in 1800 and acquired by Major Sanborn along with the surrounding farm land to establish the seminary campus prior to 1883. The principal's house remained in the same location after serving subsequent purposes for the Sanborn Regional School District. The home and barn were disassembled in 2010.

The Sanborn Seminary graduation ceremony was often held on the lawns surrounding the seminary building but was also held at the Kingston town hall at times. The 1950 commencement exercises were held at town hall and celebrated the 61st class to graduate from the seminary.

SANBORN SEMINARY
KINGSTON
New Hampshire

Commencement Exercises 1950

KINGSTON TOWN HALL
Monday, June 12

Exercises to begin at 2:30 p. m.

Sanborn Seminary offered diplomas in several areas, including business and college courses of study, such as seen on this diploma awarded to Blanche Ardella Beaulieu on June 22, 1922.

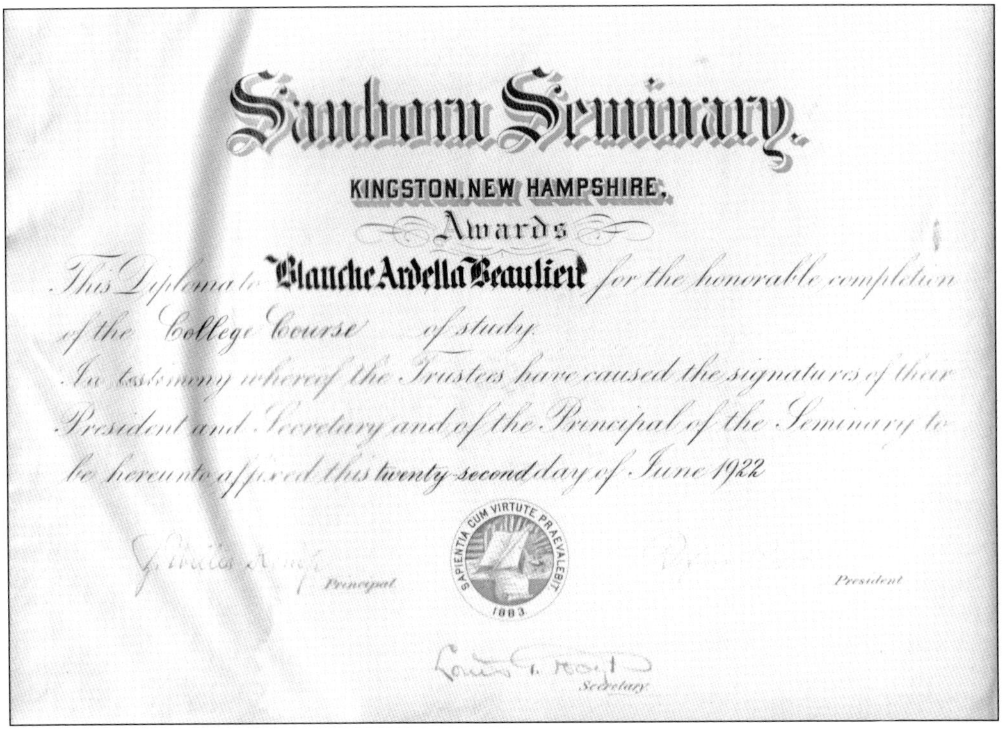

Sanborn Seminary.
KINGSTON, NEW HAMPSHIRE.
Awards
This Diploma to Blanche Ardella Beaulieu for the honorable completion of the College Course of study.
In testimony whereof the Trustees have caused the signatures of their President and Secretary and of the Principal of the Seminary to be hereunto affixed this twenty second day of June 1922

SAPIENTIA CUM VIRTUTE PRAEVALEBIT 1883

Principal

President

Secretary

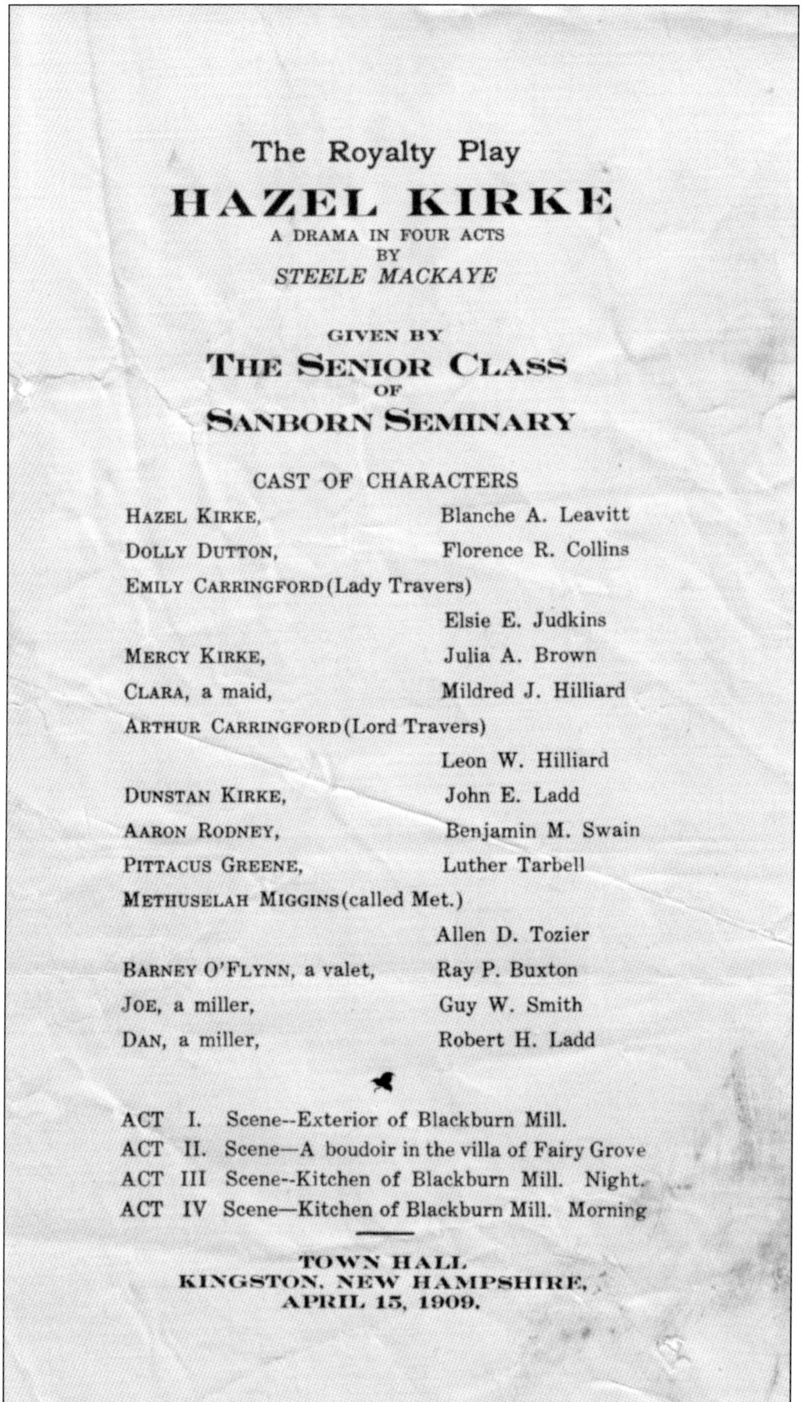

The Royalty Play

HAZEL KIRKE

A DRAMA IN FOUR ACTS
BY
STEELE MACKAYE

GIVEN BY

THE SENIOR CLASS
OF
SANBORN SEMINARY

CAST OF CHARACTERS

HAZEL KIRKE,	Blanche A. Leavitt
DOLLY DUTTON,	Florence R. Collins
EMILY CARRINGFORD(Lady Travers)	Elsie E. Judkins
MERCY KIRKE,	Julia A. Brown
CLARA, a maid,	Mildred J. Hilliard
ARTHUR CARRINGFORD(Lord Travers)	Leon W. Hilliard
DUNSTAN KIRKE,	John E. Ladd
AARON RODNEY,	Benjamin M. Swain
PITTACUS GREENE,	Luther Tarbell
METHUSELAH MIGGINS(called Met.)	Allen D. Tozier
BARNEY O'FLYNN, a valet,	Ray P. Buxton
JOE, a miller,	Guy W. Smith
DAN, a miller,	Robert H. Ladd

ACT I. Scene--Exterior of Blackburn Mill.
ACT II. Scene—A boudoir in the villa of Fairy Grove
ACT III Scene--Kitchen of Blackburn Mill. Night.
ACT IV Scene—Kitchen of Blackburn Mill. Morning

TOWN HALL
KINGSTON, NEW HAMPSHIRE,
APRIL 15, 1909.

The senior class presented the play *Hazel Kirke* on April 15, 1909. When attendance for an event was expected to be larger than the capacity in the seminary building, other venues were used for the performances. The Kingston town hall was often used for the performances, as seen on this program.

Seminary students, including several who would graduate as part of the class of 1908, are shown here on the steps of the seminary building. From left to right are (first row) unidentified, Ernest Seavers, Frankie Fellows, Bill Davis, ? Bremers, and Marion Barrett; (second row) Sybil Kemp, Fronie Jorole, two unidentified, Lyman Hoole, and Leonard Whippen.

The 1906 Sanborn baseball team included, from left to right, (first row) ? Flint, ? Warner, ? Ladd, and ? Murphy; (second row) John Elvin Tuck, Charles W. Kemp, and Roland W. Cheney; (third row) Allen G. Collins, Henry F. Judkins, principal ? Kemp, ? Burrill (captain), and Charles Collins; (fourth row) George W. Palmer, ? French, and Roy J. Carr.

The Sanborn Regional School District Planning Board, shown here in January 1965, met to consider the purchase of Sanborn Seminary. The planning board consisted of representatives of Kingston, Newton, Fremont, and Brentwood, but Fremont and Brentwood later opted out. From left to right are (first row) David Richards, Christopher Sherrill (chairman of the local board), Kenneth Briggs, Gordon Cheney of Newton, and George Harmon of Kingston; (second row) Walter Turner of Fremont, Mrs. Charles Pare of Brentwood, David Conant of Kingston, James O'Niel (state legislative consultant), and Damon Russell (administrative services director).

Three

Community

Kingston has a strong sense of community, with a wide variety of events and activities for people of all ages. Contained within the town's borders are several lakes and ponds offering many opportunities for boating, fishing, and swimming. Situated on Great Pond, Kingston State Park has been in operation since 1934 providing residents with pristine water and beautiful picnic facilities. The park also offers changing facilities and a bathhouse.

In addition to the many recreational opportunities that Kingston residents have enjoyed over the year, the community has always prided itself on its many varied clubs and organizations. Little League baseball, Pop Warner football, Girl Scouts, and Boy Scouts have all played a role in the lives of Kingston youth. The Kingston Coronet Band, the Kingston Players theater organization, and other groups have been a source of community entertainment for well over 150 years. This strong pride in Kingston continues to this day.

Whether participating in an organization or just enjoying the natural amenities that Kingston has to offer, residents have always taken the time to enjoy their small-town life. The balance between work and community continues to be an integral part of Kingston's history.

Josiah Bartlett was born in Amesbury, Massachusetts, in 1729, and was the second signer of the Declaration of Independence, after John Hancock. Bartlett moved to Kingston in 1750 and established himself as the only physician in the area. He became politically active, serving as a delegate to the Continental Congress and eventually becoming New Hampshire's first governor.

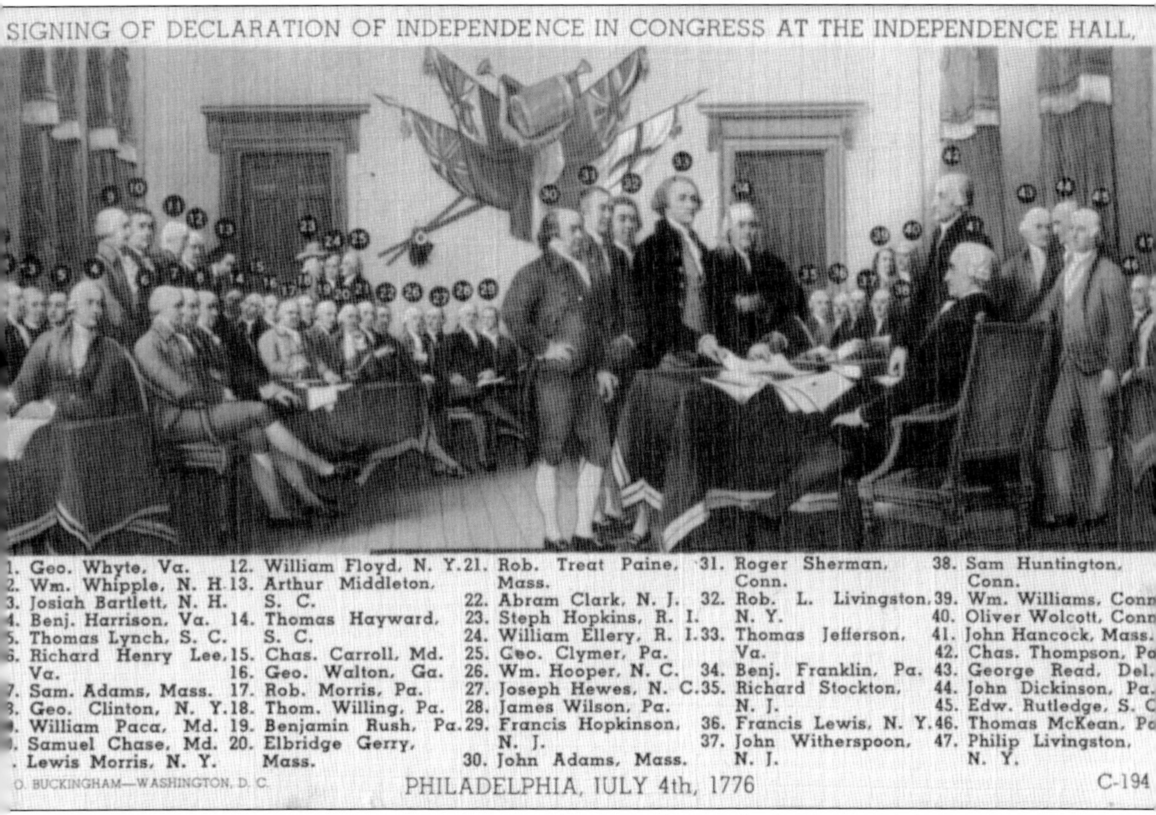

Josiah Bartlett, shown in this postcard seated third from left in the back, signed the Declaration of Independence while serving as a delegate to the Continental Congress. His political career continued after the Revolution as first governor of New Hampshire and then as a member of the New Hampshire Supreme Court, despite not having a legal background. He lived the remainder of his life in Kingston until his death on May 19, 1795.

Arthur Reynolds was a local antiques dealer and collector who purchased this cobbler's shop from an estate in Danville and moved it to his Main Street property next to his antique barn. Buildings like this were scattered throughout Kingston's backyards as many residents became involved in producing pieces for the shoe manufacturers in Kingston, Danville, and Haverhill.

The Lone Tree Scout Reservation is a 136-acre Boy Scout camp founded in 1949. Since its start, the camp has at times operated as part of the New Hampshire scouting operations and the New England scouting facilities. The camp continues to operate campsites and year-round cabins for scouting units as well as families. Available activities include boating, swimming, obstacle courses, and target ranges, including archery, as seen in this 1950s postcard. (Courtesy of James Enright.)

Brownie Troop 555 members proudly pose at their investiture in 1972. From left to right are (first row) Michelle Currier, Pamela Streeter, Kim Chamberlin, Sharon Batal, and Louise Cross; (second row) Connie Durgin, Cheryl Borin, Bonnie Mathews, Heidi Misenheimer, Wendy Brusso, and Jeannette Lamson; (third row) Cindy Jenner, Nancy Riley, Michelle Bernier, Susan Spofford, Sarena Diamond, and Joyce Sadowski; (fourth row) Debbie Sargent, Rennee McPhee, Jill Hogue, and Elizabeth Bakie. The leaders are Mrs. Charles Moore (left) and Mrs. John Tilton. (Courtesy of Seacoast Media.)

In 1972, Girl Scout Troop 318 members display the badges they had earned. From left to right are (first row) Debra Murray, Cathy Dow, and Sheryl Robie; (second row) Carol St. Onge, Alison Gould, Leanne Trombly, Debra Moore, and Jacklyn Becotte. (Courtesy of Seacoast Media.)

This man on a cart being pulled by a burro was an employee of Tom Arnold, who owned a shoe factory in Haverhill as well as a summer camp in Kingston that became Camp Treasure Lea in 1944. Arnold is in the background looking toward the camera. This photograph was taken in the early 1940s by Harry "Whiskers" Clark on the Plains.

In September 1975, Pres. Gerald Ford visited Kingston with New Hampshire US senator Louis Wyman (left) and New Hampshire governor Meldrim Thompson Jr. (right). Shown here in front of Bakie Elementary School, President Ford campaigns with Senator Wyman, who was in a close race. (Courtesy of Seacoast Media.)

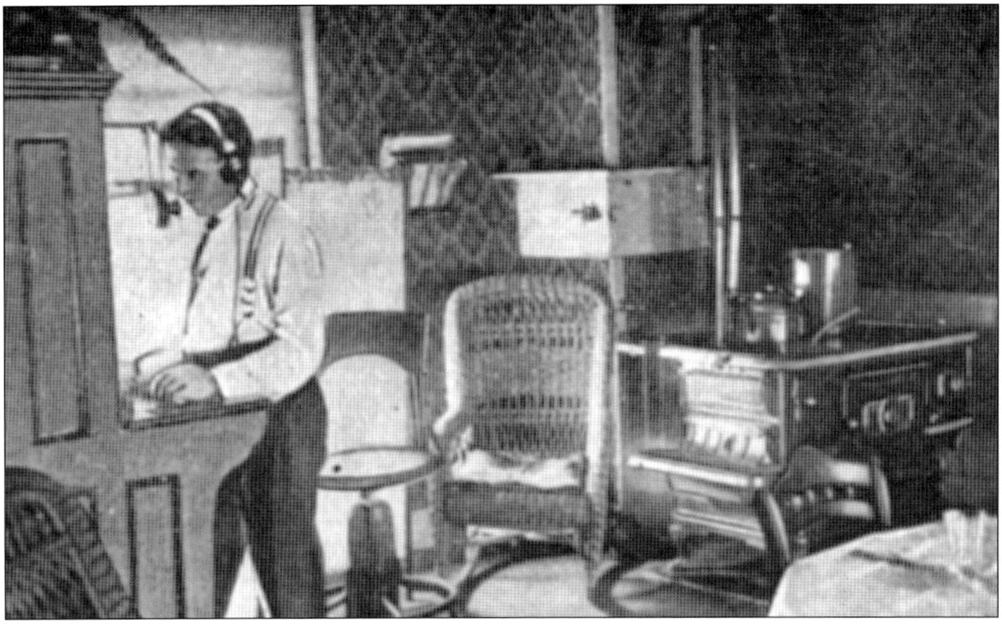

Telephone operator George Stevens played a critical role in routing calls to Kingston residents. He is seen here at the exchange in the home of his in-laws around 1911. Telephone operators often set up in their own homes, with equipment incorporated into their living area, as seen below. As the role of the telephone developed, the operators moved to other locations throughout Kingston until automation eventually took over.

The Kimball Carriage Factory complex at 6–10 Depot Street sold carriages as well as other products for horses including harnesses, ropes, and whips. The factory employees shown here in the 1880s include owner Daniel Kimball (standing fourth from right wearing suspenders). The Kimball Carriage Factory was one of many carriage factories leading Kingston to become known as the "Carriage Towne."

Unidentified visitors to Kingston State Park are shown taking advantage of the opportunity to boat on Great Pond. In addition to boating, there were many other activities popular with residents and tourists, including fishing, swimming, and a picnic area where park-goers could barbecue. Included in the nominal park entrance fee was access to a bathhouse.

A family driving by the Plains made for an opportunity for Harry "Whiskers" Clark to take a picture. Clark developed the photographs in his tent, seen here at right, using his own formula. The tent was a fixture of the Plains alongside the gazebo.

Whiskers Clark sold his photography services to the people of Kingston. His skills were well known around Kingston and he documented much of the life of the town in the first part of the 20th century. In addition to selling photographs, he also sold ice cream from his tent on the Plains.

Gordon Bakie, a 1960 graduate of Sanborn Seminary, is shown here in 1960 in his Air Force uniform. He spent three years assigned to Langley Air Force Base before being sent to Vietnam in 1963 as a flight engineer. His time in the military lasted five years, of which four were active duty and one in the reserves. Bakie continued to work with military aircraft as a civilian mechanic at Pease Air Force Base in Portsmouth for 20 years. He has served in many community organizations, including the fire department and on the Sanborn Seminary board of trustees.

The unveiling of the monument in front of town hall was well attended. Dedicated to the men and women of Kingston who served in World War II, it is engraved, "For what they were, and all they did, remember them today." The monument was donated by Andrew Christie of Christie Poultry Farms, and the dedication was held on August 10, 1946.

Andrew Christie, owner of Christie Poultry Farms, is pictured here with his son Andrew "Spizz" Christie Jr. in 1955 at the farm in Kingston. Christie was one of the earliest US poultry breeders to recognize the need to breed poultry specifically for meat-producing characteristics. He developed his own strain of the New Hampshire breed, which dominated the boiler market in the United States. Kingston was the center of the poultry industry through the 1930s and 1940s before competition from feed suppliers moved the business to southern states.

Kingston State Park, on the shores of Great Pond, has provided picnic, swimming, boating, and fishing opportunities for Kingston residents since 1934. The park currently occupies 44 acres of land with picnic facilities and water-related amenities.

Andrew Christie, shown here in 1942 at the Kingston hatchery of Christie Farms, shows daughter Jane Christie how chicks are measured and sorted. Andrew Christie and his wife, Carolyn, were involved in many Kingston organizations. The Christies donated many items important to Kingston's rich history, including the town's original charter.

The importance of the Kingston poultry industry to the national poultry supply is evident in this photograph from April 20, 1946, showing the delivery of Christie Poultry Farms chickens to Tyson Farms in Arkansas by airplane. This was the first of many such deliveries to Tyson Farms and other national poultry chains. John Tyson, pictured here at left accepting his first delivery, personally corresponded with Andrew Christie regarding the high quality of the chickens delivered.

Pictured here is a welcome home celebration for returning residents who served in World War II. From left to right are Harold Whittier, unidentified, Richard Friend, Wilbert Bergeron, Bud Ingraham, unidentified, Marvin Simes, Raymond McComb, unidentified, Robert Bowers, Edward Jendreau, Norman Winslow, Warren George, Stanton Bunker, unidentified, Wilbert Swett, Robert Rock, Frederick Teague, Robert Nichols, Frank Jewell, unidentified, Bernard Robie, unidentified, Wallace Swett, Oral Collins, Frances Kemp, Robert Barrett, Clayton Ingraham, Jack Braley, unidentified, William Greenwood, unidentified, Wilfred West, Donald Clark, Eugene Clark, Paul Clark, Elden Nason, Wesley West, unidentified, and Arnold or Leonard Philbrick. Arthur Reynolds took this photograph in 1946.

John Bakie poses in his 1930 Sanborn Seminary graduation picture. The Bakie family's presence in Kingston includes the oldest family farm in operation in town, several businesses, production of many of Kingston's early postcards, and a significant donation to establish Kingston's first elementary school to combine the previous seven district schools.

These Kingston State Park staff members in the 1930s are, from left to right, (first row) Aida Campbell, Abbie (Sue) Avery, Mildred Tucker, and Leila Collins (second row) lifeguard Kenneth Douglas, superintendent Arthur Tucker, Robert Bennett, Vernon Lewis, Richard Eustes, and lifeguard Stanton Bunker. Park staff played an important role in keeping visitors safe and providing access to park amenities. Lifeguards were stationed along the roped swimming area, while other staff members served as park rangers or worked in the bathhouse.

Den 3 of Cub Scout Pack 90 presented a skit during a meeting at the First Congregational Church in 1976. From left to right are Gary Wheelock, Andrew Richard, Tim Morgan, Kevin ?, ? Nason, and Billy Carrier, with den mother Helen Richard. (Courtesy of Seacoast Media.)

In 1983, Boy Scout Troop 93 spent a weekend camping at Lone Tree Reservation on Country Pond in Kingston. Pictured here are, from left to right, Scott Blair, Jeff Fisher, John Archambault, Brian Talham, Mike Babcock, T.J. Buttrick, Walter Fortier, Brian Currier, Dennis Pelletier, Craig Schiller (senior patrol leader), and David Mascioli (assistant senior patrol leader). Also pictured are Dick Talham (far left), Wally Pelletier (far right), and scoutmaster Jerry Mascioli (front). (Courtesy of Seacoast Media.)

Shown here in the 1930s, the Kingston State Park bathhouse included showers and changing rooms for park visitors. Additional facilities and expansions have since been added.

Camp Treasure Lea offered day and overnight camp experiences for boys and girls from New Hampshire and nearby states. Here, Jane Christie (second row, far right) and her cabin mates, along with their camp counselors, pose in the 1940s. The campers and counselors all wear their Treasure Lea camp shirts.

Camp Treasure Lea was founded by Mildred C. Crowley in 1944 and was open to boys and girls from ages four to fourteen. The camp saw children from all over New Hampshire, as well as some from out of state. Many of the local high school students stepped up to become camp counselors over their summer break and took care of all the campers during the day.

Treasure Lea campers had many different activities as part of their camp day. In this image from the 1940s, Andrew "Spizz" Christie is at far right with fellow campers riding seesaws while wearing their Treasure Lea shirts. Campers also took field trips to horse stables, along with other activities as part of their fun.

As seen in this 1930s postcard, Great Pond had a swimming area prior to becoming part of Kingston State Park. A swimming area at Great Pond continues to the present day for the enjoyment of park visitors. (Courtesy of James Enright.)

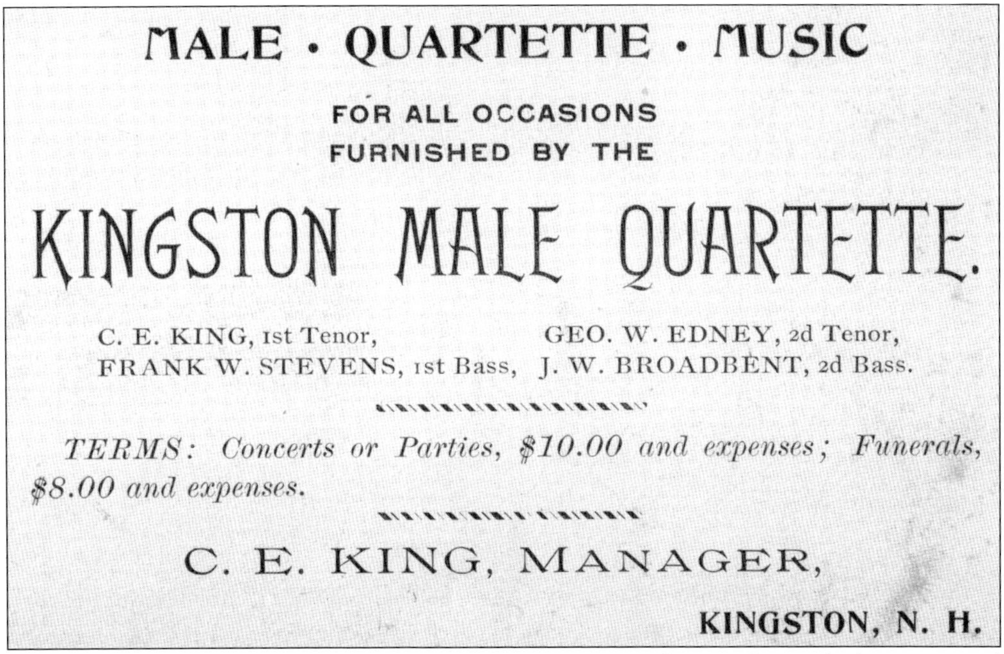

The Kingston Male Quartet was a four-person singing group performing during the late 1800s and into the early 1900s. The quartet consisted of Joseph Broadbent, Charles King, Frank Stevens, and George Edney. The group disbanded in the early 1900s, likely as a result of members having other obligations.

Shown here standing on the Plains in the 1890s is Ora Pearson. In the background on the left is the Simeon P. Clark House (currently the 1686 House restaurant) with its original barns behind it. On the right is the John T. Clark store, which sold tin products including cups, plates, toys, and others.

Living near Greenwood Pond, Earl (left) and Walter Carter enjoyed fishing and are shown here in the 1930s displaying their catch. Being close to the center of Kingston and with easy access, Greenwood Pond offers a small beach area and excellent fishing.

The Kingston Brass Band is shown here in 1886 on Great Pond as they performed for summer residents. From left to right are Clarence Cilley, Jerry Tucker, unidentified, Fred Osgood, John Webster, Edger Nichols, unidentified, Charles Flanders, Albert Nichols, unidentified, Charles Leach, Walter Clark, two unidentified, Herbert Webster, unidentified, Augustus Bragdon, and two unidentified.

At the 1946 Kingston town celebration, members of the newly formed Veteran's Club gathered for this picture. From left to right are (first row) Eugene Clark, Bob Nichols, Bob Barrett, Wilfred West, and Frank Jewell; (second row) Bill Bergeron, Don Clark, Paul Clark, Bernie Robie, and Jack Braley.

In this 1930s photograph, employees of the Bakie Brothers General Store are arriving to deliver supplies in support of flood victims in Manchester, New Hampshire. It is not known which flood the delivery was for.

David Flagg (left), Christie Poultry Farms geneticist, and Frank Field are processing New Hampshire chickens for testing in 1955. Christie's strain of the New Hampshire breed was developed in Kingston and helped launch Christie as a leader in the poultry industry. He used the word "spizzerinktum" to promote the chickens' supposed vigor.

Four

Celebrations

Since the founding of Kingston in 1694, residents have celebrated their rich history. Celebrations take place on national holidays and on the occasions of milestone anniversaries of the town's founding. Starting in the early 1990s, in preparation for Kingston's 300th anniversary in 1994, the town celebrated Kingston Days on the Plains every August.

The earliest photographs documenting Kingston are from the late 1800s and early 1900s, when people primarily traveled by carriage. As the parades and celebrations continued through the years and advancements in transportation developed, parade participants kept pace. Gradually, automobiles dominated the celebrations on the Plains. During the 1919 celebration to commemorate the town's founding and the end of World War I, the Plains served as a temporary runway for a World War I biplane as part of the festivities.

Following World War II, patriotism was strong and veterans from Kingston and surrounding towns marched in the August 6, 1946, Fourth of July parade. With the celebration focused around the center of Kingston, many of the historic homes overlooking the Plains were adorned with patriotic banners and flags.

Pride in Kingston has also been demonstrated annually with a carnival to celebrate the Fourth of July, an idea first raised in 1937 by the Firemen's Association. Beginning in 1956, the annual carnival was sponsored by the Kingston Veteran's Club, the Kingston Lion's Club, and the Firemen's Association. For many years starting in the 1930s, Kingston Days included an annual 30-foot bonfire with a car on top. The bonfire was a major attraction until the carnival ended in the 1990s. The annual celebration has also included a carnival with rides, games, and other attractions. Although the Fourth of July carnival is no longer held, that same celebratory excitement continues today with Kingston Days every August. To celebrate Kingston's 325th anniversary, the state granted Kingston's request to build a bonfire reminiscent of days gone by. Kingston residents continue to celebrate their past, and their celebrations reflect their pride.

Kingston's annual Fourth of July bonfire tradition started in the 1930s when the people of Kingston collected materials from the poultry farms to burn in the fire. Over time, the bonfires were constructed of wooden pallets, logs, or barrels. Eventually, a car was added to the top, and people would stay until the end to watch it fall. The bonfires would be around 30 feet tall, not including the car. Cars were eventually taken out of the tradition due to environmental concerns. The bonfires stopped in the late 1990s when the carnival was discontinued, but were brought back in 2019 to celebrate Kingston's 325th anniversary.

During the celebration of Kingston's 275th anniversary in 1969, buildings were proudly adorned with patriotic decorations. The market at the corner of Main and Depot Streets (formerly the Bakie Brothers General Store) is shown here decorated for the festivities. In the background, Nichols Memorial Library can be seen, also patriotically decorated.

Overlooking the Plains, Josiah Bartlett's house is seen here decorated during Kingston Days in 1969. The house was built in 1774 by Dr. Bartlett after a fire destroyed his previous home. It was recognized as a national historic landmark in 1971.

The bandstand on the Plains was also decorated to commemorate the 275th anniversary in 1969.

During the 1969 anniversary celebration, the original firehouse built in 1895 on Depot Road was decorated to celebrate. Kingston's first fire department was formed in 1883 and consisted of volunteers. This building and the 1929 town hall housed the fire department equipment until 1949, when a central fire department was constructed on the site of the former Plains School.

The Horribles Parade, held on July 4, 1915, traveled down Main Street along the Plains. As seen above, the parade included people in wagons, pushing baby strollers, and riding bikes, all of which were brightly decorated with American flags. Others joined the parade on foot. Below, a person is riding a high-wheeler bicycle along Main Street, a difficult feat on unpaved dirt roads such as this. With automobiles outnumbered by horse-drawn wagons, the roads were rough and contained lots of ruts from wagon wheels.

The 1919 225th anniversary celebration also celebrated the end of World War I. During the parade, many vehicles were decorated with flags draped over hoods and fenders, and reminders of how Kingston residents were part of the war effort. This car is carrying members of the local Red Cross unit.

One of the many parade vehicles during the 1919 celebration was sponsored by Walter S. Clark, a Kingston business that transitioned with changing times, starting with a carriage building business in the 1870s. The parade vehicle advertised Fisk Tires, which were sold at Clark's automobile repair business.

Nichols Memorial Library in the center of Kingston was one of many buildings decorated for the 1919 celebrations. The celebrations revolved around Kingston's 225th anniversary, Old Home Days, and the end of World War I. The strong pride of the Kingston residents was evident through the decorated buildings, parade, and events on the Plains.

The 1946 event included a parade to celebrate Kingston's 250th anniversary and the Allied victory in World War II. Many of the parade participants were members of the armed forces proudly wearing their uniforms and marching with flags. The Raymond American Legion group is shown here.

An ox team is shown during the 1946 parade. The farmer parading this team is likely Irving Nelson, who frequently gave children rides around the Plains in his wagon. To honor him and his contributions to the community following his death in 1973, local farmers paraded their ox teams with a hay wagon.

During the 1946 parade, Frederic Greenwood (left) and Patricia Richardson are seated in their wagon pulled by a Saint Bernard, while Esther Greenwood walks alongside.

Neighboring towns also participated in Kingston's 250th anniversary celebration, including East Kingston. The East Parish of East Kingston parade vehicle was pulled by a team of horses and featured people in period attire. The parade traveled along Main Street. Other towns participating in the parade included Fremont, Epping, and West Epping.

The Plains doubled as a runway for this World War I Curtiss JN "Jenny" biplane. It was flown in as part of the triple celebration to mark the end of World War I a few months earlier, Kingston's 225th anniversary, and Old Home Days on August 6, 1919.

The Kingston Carnival was an annual Fourth of July tradition with a bonfire at the center of the celebration, among other activities and events. Posters such as this one from the 1950s advertising "All New Space Age Rides" were posted throughout Kingston.

Neighborhood children gathered to march in the 1946 parade. Shown in their fabulous costumes are, from left to right, Cindi Bakie, Jane Auger, Donald Sanborn, Kitty Long, Butch Long, Dottie Long, Lee Decatur, Gordon Bakie, Dale Winch, Sandra Winch, Jean Beals, and Barby Friend.

Seen here during the 275th anniversary parade in 1969, Don and Priscilla Clark were dressed in historical attire on their way to attend the Firemen's Ball.

At the 1919 celebration, residents from across the town gathered in front of town hall to celebrate. A wide variety of transportation can be seen above parked on the Plains, from horse and buggies to early automobiles. To keep the horses from becoming frightened, it was customary for them to be separated from automobiles at events such as this. In addition to this large gathering of people on the Plains below, there was a parade that traveled along Main Street.

During the 1969 parade, Kingston constructed a float to honor the first governor of New Hampshire, Josiah Bartlett, with participants dressed in period attire. The float is shown making its way along Main Street around the Plains.

As part of the 1969 parade, the Kingston Fire Department drove Smokey Bear on its 1930s fire truck. This also happened to be Smokey Bear's 25th anniversary, having first appeared in campaigns to prevent forest fires in 1944. His slogan "Only you can prevent forest fires" was first used in 1947.

The First Congregational Church celebrated the 1969 anniversary with decorations adorning its windows and doors. In close proximity to the Plains, the church was certainly visible to parade attendees and others celebrating Kingston's founding.

The 1686 House is Kingston's oldest house, seen here decorated for the 225th anniversary celebration in 1969. The building still has its original wide pine floorboards and hand-cut beams. Although originally built as a residence overlooking the Plains, it was converted to a restaurant in 1972 and is still in operation.

The annual Kingston Carnival was a great way for residents to celebrate the Fourth of July. During the years when the bonfire was held, elaborate structures were built to support an automobile (with the engine removed), as seen in this poster from the 1960s or 1970s. The event was sponsored for many years by the Kingston Veteran's Club, Kingston Lion's Club, and Kingston Fire Department.

Kingston celebrations were sometimes announced with banners, as seen in this late 1800s view of the intersection of Main Street and Depot Road looking north. The Bakie Brothers General Store is on the right.

Clark's Garage built a float for the 1919 Fourth of July parade. Shown here along the Main Street route, the driver is pulling a wagon filled with bicycles, car parts, and other miscellaneous items representing the long history of Walter S. Clark and Sons.

During the 1969 parade, a newly acquired 1968 class A pumper truck leads older firefighting equipment from the 1950s. Residents lined Main Street to watch the parade.

During the 1919 parade, these residents decorated their automobile to celebrate. The parade traveled through downtown. Many turned out for the 225th anniversary parade to celebrate Kingston's founding, Old Home Days, and the end of World War II.

About the Kingston Historical Museum

On August 6, 2019, Kingston celebrated the 325th anniversary of the founding of the town. Since its founding in 1970, the Kingston Historical Museum has been sharing the history and cultural heritage of Kingston's earliest inhabitants to the present generation. The museum is headquartered in the historic 1898 Nichols Memorial Library at 169 Main Street. The museum complex includes Kingston's original firehouse, tramp house, cobbler shop, and Grace Daley barn, which houses its collection of carriages.

The majority of the photographs that appear in this book are from the museum's collection gathered over the last 50 years. We thank all of our donors and the people of Kingston, without whom the museum would not be possible. It was our pleasure to work with Jim, Kalena, and Emma to bring these images of our beloved hometown to readers.

—Lesley-Ann Hume and Walt Roy

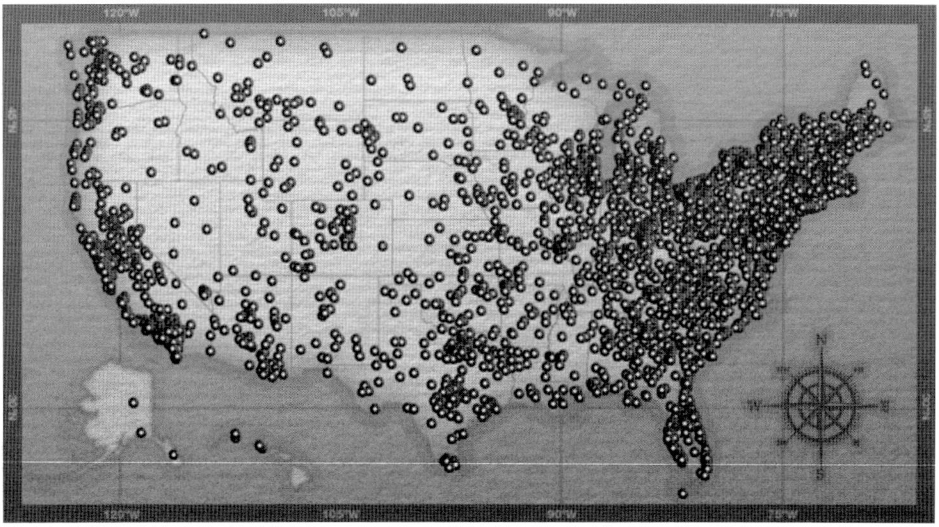